DEAR ALL

Also by Michael Gottlieb

Letters To A Middle Aged Poet
The Dust
Memoir And Essay
The Likes Of Us
Lost And Found
Careering Obloquy
Gorgeous Plunge
More Than All (with Ted Greenwald)
The Night Book
The River Road
Valu Pac
New York
The Blue Slope
Pantographic
96 Tears
Local Color/Eidetic Deniers

DEAR ALL

Michael Gottlieb

ROOF BOOKS
NEW YORK

ISBN: 978-1-931824-50-7
Library of Congress Card Catalog No. 2013931837

Cover and author photo by Isabel Gottlieb

Art by James Siena
Geared Pathway, 2011, graphite on paper, photograph by Kerry Ryan McFate,
courtesy Pace Gallery, page 8
Shaded Connected Hooks—long way l'ile du Levant, 2007, graphite on paper,
photograph courtesy the artist and Pace Gallery, page 40
shaded connected hooks, 2007, graphite on paper, photograph by G.R. Christmas,
courtesy Pace Gallery, page 72

ACKNOWLEDGEMENTS
Thanks to the editors of the following publications in which some of
these poems originally appeared: *The Brooklyn Rail*, *Boog City Reader*,
Bumpers/Cuneiform Press, *Critiphoria*, *Otoliths*, *Summerstock*

 This book was made possible, in part, with public funds from the
New York State Council on the Arts, a state agency.

Roof Books are distributed by
Small Press Distribution
1341 Seventh Avenue
Berkeley, CA. 94710-1403
Phone orders: 800-869-7553
www.spdbooks.org

Roof Books
are published by
Segue Foundation
300 Bowery
New York, NY 10012
seguefoundation.com

ONE

IS THERE ANY SUCH THING AS SALVAGE 11
GO BIG 12
I'M JUST SAYING 13
SEVEN AGAINST THEMES 14
NO FRENEMIES ON THE LEFT 15
BIG BOX ESCHATALOGY 16
ALL OF YOUR SURGICAL SUPPLY NEEDS 17
WE DWELL IN THE LOWER CASE 18
SINGLE SERVE PACKET 19
A FLYING SQUAD 20
FROM YOUR MOUTH TO MAGOG'S EAR 21
REDUCED IN PRINCIPAL 22
THE HEAVEN BENEATH OUR FEET 23
A MUST-AVOID 24
RENT SEEKING FOR THE REST OF US 25
INFORMATIONAL SESSION 26
IF LIONEL WAS ONLY A TRAIN 27
THE ASCENDING CHORDS OF THE DULCET FARFISA 28
OUT OF SOMEWHERE 29
THE REPRISED DEMISE 30
MY PEN HAS A NAME IT'S A PEN NAME 31
THE FURTIVE MOVEMENTS 32
AIR-COOLED 33
FEBRILE AND LURID 34
YOU HYPERVIGILANTE YOU 35
WHERE DOES THIS LEAVE US 36
HERE AT THE LAST TRANCHE 37
IT WAS ALL SO WELL FOUNDED 38
THE DEMURE THANATOS 39

TWO

ADVANCE AND BE RECOGNIZED 43
WHAT GOES WITHOUT SAYING 46
WHO BETTER THAN 48
FORGETTING TO TAKE 50

POETRY THE GATEWAY DRUG *52*

UNSAFE HARBOR *55*

THE STIRRING SENTIMENT *58*

THE COOLING WELTS *61*

FUN FACTS *64*

I DIDN'T SEE THAT COMING *65*

THE WRETCHED OF THE EARTH TONES *67*

THIS I FIND HARD TO BELIEVE *68*

WE ARE UNHAPPY TO SERVE YOU *69*

THREE

AND WE SHALL NEVER SPEAK OF THIS AGAIN *75*

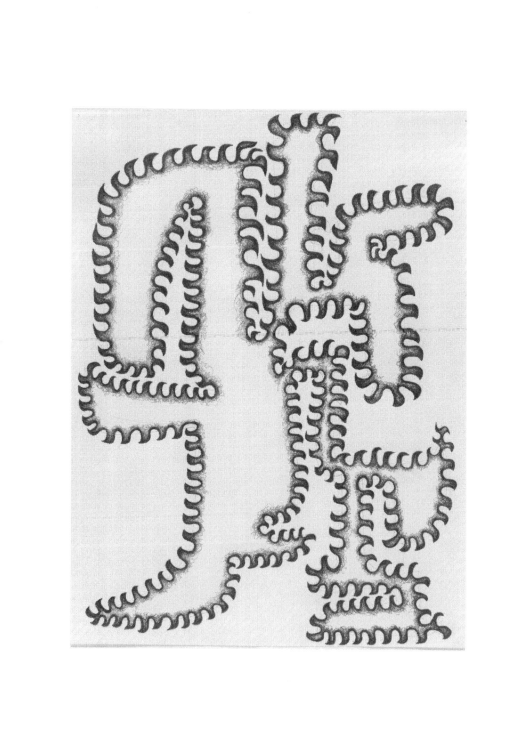

ONE

IS THERE ANY SUCH THING AS SALVAGE

our whorls
have done us wrong
again

and still we swear fealty

to tergiversation
this salvation of the callow

you have too much mass
you always did

a foreclosure a clearance
a haircut for the investors
a really nice reorg
a debulking

foregrounding
is not all that is left

yes
you have more
to tell
and show

GO BIG

this is
the ground attack

go big go long go home
fail quickly

I know you can explain to me
how it is
that we don't all
end up like this

in this black arts and crafts supply company

if only the after-life
was more like the after-party

the rammed earth shifting beneath our feet

I'M JUST SAYING

what stirs
drawing near
dragging its club

a hemmed and altered exhaust
trailing you
like some anathematic footer

balefully unabashed

I'm pushing all this along the funnel
it's a nurturing story
it's in my pipeline

since you need to ask

you too shall be restored
or maybe restocked

SEVEN AGAINST THEMES

an ill-gotten loss

a high-functioning

because
there is no one else
who can walk with you
down this road

it is a love
that dares not speak
its middle name

the very name
makes markets

making the perfect
the enemy of the good
n plenty

you don't

NO FRENEMIES ON THE LEFT

indicted perhaps
convicted never

it's upping sticks
and lighting out

it's a frosty
mug's game

an impure lack of thought

not just reckless
eyewateringly cock-eyed

a stymie

a self-styled

not enough
already

BIG BOX ESCHATALOGY

taking arms to the encroaching hordes of reconciliation

the unavoidable dealings with those who
don't recognize they are your betters

shot through with that ineffable sense of bilious enlightenment

pre-lapsarian home improvement
in the original garden apartment
as if there was a difference
between evicted and expelled

when at long last we are presented
with the keys to the suburbs

when we finally get to burn the title

ALL OF YOUR SURGICAL SUPPLY NEEDS

a low-down liar

a true-up

what are we to make of you

you with those eyes
at the side of your head

a catch in the throat
at the feast of unreason

it's time for us once again
to swing into unease

WE DWELL IN THE LOWER CASE

the less than keenly awaited news

there was so much more
I was prepared for you to say

still unsettled along the shore

I see it all
when I close my eyes

the flashing poles
the mounting missings
the undeserved rest
the mendacious double clutching
the stuttering time travel

it's like this
you don't need to know how to drive
in order to get car sick

SINGLE SERVE PACKET

rounding this latest headland

like all of the sunny suppositions
we once argued long and hard for

before us now stretch
the caking the rivulets the swotting the graven
the semi-defeated routing
the hemostitches the soiled gavottes
the deposed affirmations
serving one and all to remind us

of this distracted last stand
where those who in our own way we would call
the unchurched among us
discover their comparative disadvantage

this
your own personal
heat sink

A FLYING SQUAD

this shrug

that hub

those slim volumes

over-reaches
in Centereach

vouchsafing
for anyone   .

FROM YOUR MOUTH TO MAGOG'S EAR

as you were

as of this writing

another member
one of those uncaring professions

a maximum follower

a whole parade

a knock-on effect

REDUCED IN PRINCIPAL

effortless effervescence
ground down to gristly refutation

behind the airless arcade
a condemned cul de sac

there I was wearing a suit

we found ourselves
last among equals

how incapable were we
of putting our money on anything else

it was so very impressive
how little you missed

and how lucky I was
to escape
as whole as I did

THE HEAVEN BENEATH OUR FEET

a piercing cry
from the dark of the fen

from one we'd long deemed
a frank no-account

now we know that
counting is not the same thing
as mensuration

we find ourselves
demasted once again
thrown upon those old familiars

doesn't all this imprudence owes us
at least one happy error

since we know
there is no such thing
as a natural cause

A MUST-AVOID

you snatch the sceptre
from the nerveless hand

in and among
that place
where we are free to do our worst

a barrens of your own

the sensible resistance
to posing for the group picture

there must needs be this awful majesty
in the command you assumo

there are doings
and then there are deeps

where once we were washed
from the Corniche

RENT SEEKING FOR THE REST OF US

we know how to take a punch
we should
with all that practice

our lies are
superb and pillowy

this too
to borrow a term from knife-play
falls within the lungeable area

how much are we allowed to ask
of each other
and how often

bracing for a whole lot
of nothing

that which goes wheels-up
when it comes time for toes-up

AN INFORMATIONAL SESSION

here at the dawn of
the lack of volition

to uplift and tease apart
this is what we were put on this earth to do

as if we could ever prefer the built world over the unbuilt word

on the way to the exemplarily emptied cities
the sad purser shuffles among the showroomed stipulations

once they land
and reveal themselves as gods
what do we do with them

IF LIONEL WAS ONLY A TRAIN

you must be exhausted
what with killing your father and sleeping with your mother

if it's just a situational lack of awareness
it isn't necessarily time to consider sundowning you

what paid versus owned versus earned
really means in this flyblown bazaar
this marketplace of unattended ideas

the bar we've set is low
that's why we like drinking here with you

THE ASCENDING CHORDS OF THE DULCET FARFISA

the star-crossed triumphalist
looks upon his works

remind me again
what it is I'm trying to forget

the freighted remains
of the future

don't get me wrong

I'm so very good at doing that

all by myself

OUT OF SOMEWHERE

jet-assisted

full of beans

under your own power

a kind of unholy triangulation

what is it that doesn't speed up
as it approaches the ground

and now it is our turn to
ring-fence the innuendo

which was
once a combo plate
of the hit-or-miss and the baseless

back then a fair dab hand
at feigning carelessness

we try to avert our gaze
when we hear
his call and respond

look upon this man
a frank face plant now
every limb akimbo

THE JUSTICE NO ONE CARES FOR

the dun transports in a column
idling before the municipal swimming pool

a haze beneath the flyover

we call them like we don't see them

the so-called fader
the trusty old room-broom

where you were supposed to enter
where it was all said to begin
where we used to play at bombardment

the former constitutive republics of this proposition
standing forth now in all their shambles

warring delusions all along
like hereditary foemen
their eternal animus briefly papered over
in an interlude of false bonhomie

what all progressive peoples call out for

as is well known

MY PEN HAS A NAME IT'S A PEN NAME

we're all big boys now

and we want to believe
a name on the door
means a Bigelow on the floor

by all rights
we should have been evicted
from this last patch
when you showed up
now so long ago
your own lease must be expiring soon

and contrary to what
we used to argue
it is not mere peccancy

here the big wind up
gets its own send up

and reminds us of the notional value
of a sharp pointed stick

THE FURTIVE MOVEMENTS

what we really mean
when we say
artistic differences

one whose gaze we cannot avoid
pointedly lounging
in the departure hall
another erstwhile carefree sponger

the way we get confused
when we sense
too much similitude

this one fancied himself man enough
to hew the marble with his own hands
but unlike Canova
being of only negligible strength
that afternoon in the dust-choked quarry
nearly died when he tried

the reeling receptors
so easily discomposed

and when it is our turn
will we have the pep?

AIR-COOLED

the problem pictures
a farrago of them
like fugitive cargo
secreted beneath decks
they will always be with us

as we come to grasp
why really there is no such thing
as a relief map

it starts with a lazy eyeful
a stack of incompatibilities
lowing and lowering

and we are left with
these unaided questions
these shifts of inanition
this inadvertently brusque pruning

a laugh track of prioritization

where is the awkward squad
when we need them

FEBRILE AND LURID

as if you were
equally indulgent
with the condiments
as the curare

for a long time
we thought we knew
what we were about

what you do without telling me
because you don't want to upset me

a blue thought
in a blue room
waiting for the code blue

now comes the young Lothar
once the least among us
delivering more thought leadership

a heedless glance
a pitilessly leveling edged-weapon
scraping away at what we used to hold close

YOU HYPERVIGILANTE YOU

his prosody
one disavowal
for every three vowels

all of this regrowth
would be nothing short of miraculous
if only we didn't know
the reason why

it's only natural that you should feel this way

we all need something
to do with our hands
and our mouths

what we have left to spare
a grinning reminder
rising over the inaccessible wood

a kind of po-faced maypole
we were so fain
to dance about
in our day

WHERE DOES THIS LEAVE US

too many interjections

like the fruits
of a misspent youth

backing up
to run over that reflection in the pool
one more time
just to make sure

it happens to the best of us

if you don't look on the bright side
it is just another bright shiny thing

but these are not magic beans

and words don't fail
they get a D –

HERE AT THE LAST TRANCHE

someone is always asking
for particulars
in this great indoors

it is a rump party

it is a simple syrup
composed of equal parts
infamy and indolence

that is why there is no such thing
as a bill of materials

the unadorned fastener
once the underpinning of a great industry

strait and unacknowledged
like nothing so much as
a dishonored prophet among his own

we're so used to
boiling the ocean

for good reason

IT WAS ALL SO WELL FOUNDED

I tried to keep the offering
at least a little hidden

I was really hoping
for some guy wires

I wanted one
of those nice-to-haves
for once

I tried to say
I honestly don't know
where to begin

but we certainly wished you well

casuistry
would have been so easy
for someone like you

you are
a caution
to the rest of us

you are
just a little heater

aren't you

THE DEMURE THANATOS

a wordel for the rest of us
while we wait to board

back then we assumed
it was the end of salad days
what did we know

now we know
not all words are the same size

it is a sobering thought
one of which you for one
can always use

take it like the man
you never were

to think
you have finally reached
your connecting flight

this is the distillate

this the merciless poise

TWO

ADVANCE AND BE RECOGNIZED

tonite
we are here to honor
a great poet
and a great humanitarian

an upending enthusiasm

unhelpful and detached

a gauzy emotion

letting nature
take its course

in what some might suggest
is no more than a failure
to reanimate

all the while
I am trying
to think
impure thoughts

and next time
I'm bringing
my friends

one fell
global delete

one-offs
having at it
in the torn clouds

overblown, the

mooted, the

the dismal swamp

the empty Laslo

the Telstar
which was our friend

the here and
body blows
applicator-free
and among them
them over-oxygenated maroons

roostering up
finally

"he is
good for nothing
except
target practice"

a footfall

withals

riddled

wheels like as to coming off

how the seemly
falls into the waylaid

this gambling hell

now or here

WHAT GOES WITHOUT SAYING

looking
alive

troublemakers
likely noisemakers
not unlike drawn curtains
parsing for fully-dressed

fickle on
Lake Constance

a blem
a graybar
a limpid
a layabout
a sealed train of thought

we are lowered
into the depths

we arrive
at your side

we take
a reading

and, just so, the miserablist bloc
praying to recalcitrance

for best results

some sort of outcry

overly-familiar

some sort of
logy swim-lane

this oh-so variety
decommissioning

an accompaniment

this
gimlet-eyed Gretchen

what's a bit rich

what goes
without saying

WHO BETTER THAN

who is
too big to fail?

the hazard lights
twig us

it's a kind of a
reminder-cum-temblor

recalling to mind
that we too are
as unsafe as houses

past performance
is no refuge
in bonneville

among the rough vessels

10-15 Marginal Street
asks
another essay question

a jump at the pump
leads to grisly discoveries

a rolling boil

the legitimist unrests

once bound over for trial

a right bastard

a true bill

FORGETTING TO TAKE

forgetting to take
the occasional breath

a kind of
space heater
which is interested
in your tissues

adducing
from

a squallish changeling

with no
get-go

the embarrassing dread

the proximates
the surly looks

the cringe-making
we can only
guess at

sleeping rough
on the tiles

the refiners' pact
leads to
just more

under the bridge

animal husbandry

"who is this
for... really?"

rough hewers

witless
(in McCandless)

a manifest

who is
most at home
when alone
in a crowd
(we are so)

the furious meandering

POETRY THE GATEWAY DRUG

a once-famous alto break

a naming convention making out
with itself

the king of prussia
of
unique selling propositions

in and among
the on-ramps

so sad and bendy

one too many own-goals

the recently-demapped
boulevard

(the) five Nines
the five Whys
the question behind the question

an industrial-arts
life study
class

that low ledge
that coping
the parking structure
with ready access

a dead-man's curve

without guard-rails

a sleeve
of tip-off

an analogous not-here

a robust startle reflex

stranger danger

this fold and draw
this excluded mean
confounding all science

I used to be even
stupider

spry cottagers
apple-cheeked
and conspiring

an honor bar
militating against us

Stuart The Many-Armed
The Destroyer

we are all spelunkers here
are we not

beefy and truckling

bringing the text-wrapping breaks
home in their kraft paper
with those modest corners

proceeding head-down

a safety match
insensate bismuth

crying havoc

strange Palatino

these not-yours

a referred pain

an upland note

those almighty proverbial flights to quantity

dismorphic drink-order

some sharp work at the crossroads

UNSAFE HARBOR

news you can use

the forcible touching

this dopey p.o.v.

the single contributor

the way that
all knowledge is liable

ankling

somewhat weedy
when it came to those truths

stricken with years

call to inaction

there
I'll say it again

this chariot
named Juggernaut

this brocaded facade

this city
and its aerodrome

whiffing at the
shambolic at-bat

demobbed
creedal
gunning
invective

hedgerow
caveated boreal
sham convalescent
unspeak

received patois disorderly as

this Satan with bed head

your set point

git as sick-making

the risk shed

and nothing less
bumwash

the grandees
of the local
extractive industries

this (lately) lumpen behavior

the overdetermined

renegade
provincial
seating the

a good

climb down

our fairest hope –
an ATM of assonance

our last
remit

bite your tongue
– both forks

trial-sizing

king
me

THE STIRRING SENTIMENT

a finisterre
a boiler

a great clumsy fist

pledges to the
contrary

maintenance
that skirmish

Kesar Sosa orders
a samosa

the sacred disembarkment
we would do well to forget

modesty as a foil
in mayhem

resting uncomfortably

the cheerlessly livid

the picture of rude health

breaking camp

the stone fruits

kind of like a swirly for your career

the heroic misgivings

of the poorly shod traveler

supplementary among blinkered shortfalls

this *is* my resting expression

the dazzle nutters

"I too love a well-managed slub"

a good place to grow up
a great place leave

the treason of the clerks

the torpors

shoring up the

the lack of rigor setting in

immaterial fly-blown

applying the reason

"I don't dwell on my problems
I dwell in them"

rueing
mongrelized
making light

baton charge
rackety set-asides
authorization scheming
another proper cock-up

the ginning ups

the way they say
you can get used to anything

your bitter swimmers

if there's no interest
there's no conflict

absolute goods
and services

your
pill

THE COOLING WELTS

it may come down to
some of their 'I' statements

intractable and blandishing

those back-lit cumulus
the shafts of sun

I am here to tell you that
by threatening violence
your planet faces danger
you risk obliteration
the decision rests with you

a bulb goes off
it appeals to
your bluffer self

it is a voluptuary apparent

it is wire fraud

or an addled tondo

a full rig

a precis of mortification

a blown rose
the king in his bouncy castle
the rugged double-cross
the wordless songs

the awards in
our frequent liar program

a pitch-pipe a fact-pattern a strangelet

a highly cordial detestation

this standing water

the indelible punctum

wishing you were not here

the unreliable
the given names
the endowment effect
the fighting monk

as we now know
we know nothing about you

the enactment
the yips
the familars
the special needs
this confiscatory rates

putting paid to

the night he got thrown out of Puffy's
thus joining the immortals
along that stretch of Hudson St.

the teachable rictus

the usurper Benny

should we
this moment
happen upon

how I went
from 'never' to
'from strength to strength'

gracious means full-of-grace

vicious means full-of-vice

FUN FACTS

strength
through
joylessness

speaking truth
to the power strips

it needs be said

by force
of our lack
of personality
by dint

a fight song
for those among us
with no fight
left in us

anent

an adverse selection

the kind of thing
you never want to see

all else
being unequal

I DIDN'T SEE THAT COMING

nothing says
XXXXXXXXXXXXX
like
XXXXXXXXXXXXX

honor bar

bottom of mind

bromide

testamentary

self-sowing

an artist's rendering

a white paper

addressable

helpings

a most-favored nation

a surfeit of lack
of caution

root and branch

it's hard to explain

packed with color

and moment

it is everything I wish I didn't want

having roved
there once
but no longer

like you
I'm an unfree
radical

I also have
a fair weather friend
in the lord

the offender

the forced air

the multi-purpose room

THE WRETCHED OF THE EARTH TONES

of even date

claiming
all numbers
are irrational

an ignoble gas

task lighting

it always seemed
to be the right time
to cull the poets

the thought –
we were at our best
when we were undressed

under
starter's orders

like a
Shriner with
a shiner

descending
flight risks

decamping

I don't mind
if I don't

THIS I FIND HARD TO BELIEVE

the difference between
free and necessary
acts

among the membership
of the slip and fall bar

we call for
another punitive
expedition

an intransigent
plush toy

it is the lowlands
of terra haute

it is a slippery slope
in incline, nevada

it is all about
not harshing
my jello

to be on
those back foot
caught

WE ARE UNHAPPY TO SERVE YOU

since
before

you see
before you

the full
battle rattle
of
the last past
the gate

the hiving off

all the right
title and
interest

the radio silence

the hour of power

your permanent record

darkness is not
your friend

(don't) sit
(don't) stay

a sickroom

at the impasse

Arnold Stang

this one
deserves everything
that is not
coming to it

sleeping soft
waking rough

you and your confederates

it is a rags
to rags story

tell don't show

making the
worst of it

we all need the crevice tool

the puling

the gobbets

awry

in fine

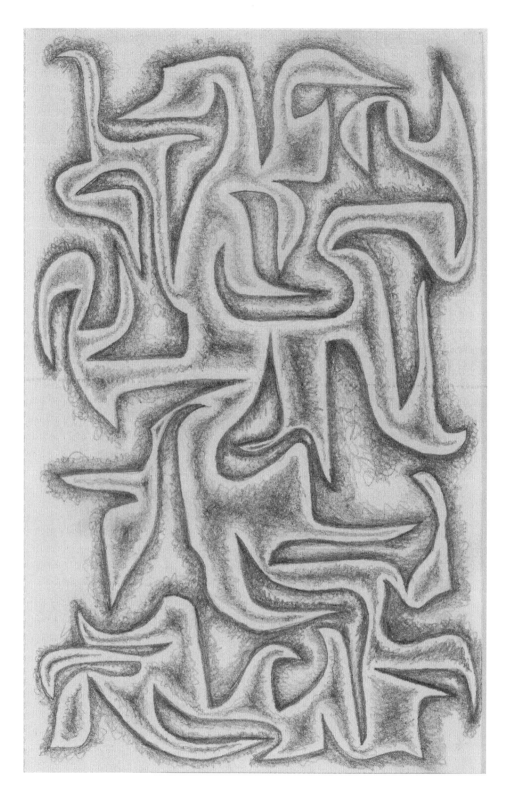

THREE

AND WE SHALL NEVER SPEAK OF THIS AGAIN

and we shall never speak of this again

bygones   not the useless idiots   neither their
novel defenses

a Completely Automated Public Turing Test To Tell Computers
and Humans Apart

a 'real big' climb down

 [JUNK] give love in action this valentine's day

an effect, whether therapeutic or adverse, that is secondary to
the one intended

headache

Hello Michael Gottlieb (logout) This is the Overview Screen of your
Expurgate Quarantine Account. From this screen you can manage
your account settings

it could turn out to be a really breathtaking take-away

facial flushing

you are not gone   but you are forgot

as poets, what *don't* we improve into a failure?

[JUNK] Turn your bedroom life into a volcano of pleasure.

boiling the ocean, that's your job   hang rustlers,
not ornaments

[JUNK] Solving ALL love making problems in a matter of
few minutes

[JUNK] Your wife need your attention? Solve all the problems with IT.

[JUNK] Top-of-the-line pilules at low prices.

feel free   to say   check please   I was born at night
just not last night

Indigestion or upset stomach

Stuffy or runny nose (rhinitis)

have you heard this one?

[JUNK] For those who want to satisfy their women.

kismet and karma—foes to the end

this is what shame   what humiliation looks like

now I need to tell you these   I'm going to my happy place

Inflammation of the sinuses (sinusitis)

and what am I supposed to do   with these information

apt   radar   unpacking   a suit of....

HUNTBURT THAT   THITZED NICATION   Accidental injury

POSITE SINDENG   BROOKS FORPBOR

an aspirational poverty   this affordable froideur   it all comes
to *this?*

76

[LIKELY JUNK] Mittel gegen Impotenz

[JUNK] Release your fantasies tonight.

[JUNK] You want to impress your girlfriend tonight?

it is an umami of perdition

Increased levels of creatine kinase in the blood (an enzyme normally found in muscles and the brain)

I don't want to know   is different than   I don't want

partial-least-squares   amok

[JUNK] Your private xxx life will be so good that you won't help from boasting it

while I appreciate the attention, howsoe'er begot   I don't want this anymore

[JUNK] Find a Russian wife here.

the overland route to these settee   the branching

Look, a B-24 Glissando ECT machine

Who Might Be a Candidate to Receive ECT?

ECT is most commonly prescribed for severe depression, where symptoms include:

Sad, blue, low mood

Altered appetitive with weight changes

Changes in sleep patterns

Low energy

Poor concentration

Decreased interest in things that once gave you pleasure

Feelings of hopelessness and/or helplessness

Feelings of guilt

Increased worrying

When is ECT necessary

ECT is a treatment for patients for whom more traditional treatments like medications have not worked,and is sometimes considered as the first choice of treatment in cases involving severe psychotic depression, malnutrition, and pregnancy

a dent   jellying

[JUNK] For sure, you will feel more pleasure after of a short course of enhancing.

[JUNK] Show her who the REAL man is

it is my practice at this hour to read some improving book

do you have that lack-of-feeling   the way I do

PACKS ERSTRY

Nausea

Dizziness

Back pain

discards

[JUNK] Your Degree shipped by Fed-Ex

this may be a sign of a rare but fatal brain disease

I'll see your trunk   the debut of _____   played hell
with _____

the lunging   an unholy

may generate unusual dreams

some loss-absorbing capacity

rarely including Headaches Facial Flushing Indigestion, known as
dyspepsia

Nasal congestion

Urinary tract infections (UTI)

you shall know them   making sure to give the people what they
don't want

they make a dessert and call it peace

[LIKELY JUNK] Votre Apoteke en ligne

[JUNK] Degree = success!

[JUNK] How about Russian bride?

at the time of writing   a mitre   this far and no ore

[JUNK] We offer the best alarm-clocks for your small friend
down there.

[JUNK] We are not greedy, come and pick as many inches as you
want. Be a confident owner and user of a mega tool! Your bedroom
got cold and you think you know the reason? If you blame your
little size for everything, stop doing it and start doing something to
increase both the dimensions and the passion in bed.

[JUNK] Women form queue, when you got as much night energy as
this Don Juan maker gives!

there's a Rule of Threes   And you, you were too

[JUNK] If there will be only girls around, will you be ready?

community property   light, or blurred vision

Diarrhea

Dizziness

Unexplained rash

commingle   a cache

do you often experience the sensation of a dry mouth?

there is the demonstration effect   for ten years running
unbefitting

an incurious admixture   where explanations   apology
defiance   self-pity   where apposites attract

'suicidal thoughts or acts'

there are net promoters and there are gross detractors

vision problems, including trouble telling the difference
between blue and green, increased sensitivity to

please don't say that this is a_____

[JUNK] Make your buildup fantastic

[JUNK] IT consultant of perfect love making art.

[JUNK] Facing a love-making problem? We will solve all your
problems in few minutes.

CORICIAS, CRUPENT

[LIKELY JUNK] Potenzprobleme - ab heute nicht mehr

Prior to taking to taking this medication, you should tell your health-
care provider if you have:

Heart disease, such as angina, congestive heart failure, or irregular
heartbeats Kidney disease or kidney failure Liver disease or liver
failure A history of a heart attack, stroke, or life-threatening
arrhythmia within the past three months Retinitis pigmentosa, which
is a rare eye problems Sensations of moral superiority A history of
severe vision loss, including a condition called NAION

you are too small for your britches   a single version of
the truth

[JUNK] the same as men look at women's breasts first, women look
at men's little friend down there first. And if they don't find there
something they like, they will never go to be with you.

[JUNK] Would you like to have as many women so you could forget their names? All that would possible if you added some extra inches to your beef stick. Just ask us how and we will help.

[JUNK] Make your intruder the best for her.

a characteristic   a vagrant   a sunshine state

that's all there is, there where no more   afeared

the sacking of Schenectady   satisfaction, as a mission statement

Contact your doctor immediately if you experience

Stomach ulcers

Other bleeding problems

Low blood pressure (hypotension)

High blood pressure (hypertension)

Sickle cell anemia

Multiple myeloma

Leukemia

it's poetry's biggest night

why is no one stepping up to mend this dangerous situation? this dubbing

[JUNK] Greater tool is easy to get

[JUNK] Make your girl happy with the help of your tool!

[JUNK] We will not let your manhood retire so soon.

[JUNK] We know the way to get your small friend up.

[JUNK] Being hung as a horse is more than possible.

what's not to love

Because of a significant risk of agranulocytosis, a potentially life-threatening adverse event this medication should be reserved for use in (1) the treatment of severely ill patients with schizophrenia who fail to show an acceptable response to adequate courses of standard antipsychotic drug treatment, or (2) for reducing the risk of recurrent suicidal behavior in patients with schizophrenia or schizoaffective disorder who are judged to be at risk of reexperiencing suicidal behavior.

the contrasty

[JUNK] Your wife need your attention? Solve all the problems with IT.

if I could grow a moustache   it *is* throwback punctuation
the stink was upon him

ONSERIO CONCLUSION

[JUNK] What's Your Hall of Shame

this addressable universe

what Captcha taught me

[LIKELY JUNK] Do it, it is possible!

that ringing in your ear   those are the bells of hell

who will care, even five years, five minutes from now?

my cookies   I miss you already   I do so have things

you are not part of the audience   you are too shirt

[JUNK] Re: She moaned in pleasure

for a limited time

Side effects rarely occurring include

Confusion

Depression

Sleep problems

Severe anxiety

Muscle tension

Involuntary teeth clenching

Nausea

Blurred vision

Faintness

Chills or sweating

Aversion to bottled water

you have no idea   there *will* be another flood   and it won't
take a hundred years

[JUNK] Power drillo won't be flaccid!

don't do your part   it's like coming to a knife fight with a flan

"Hello, junk"

ONSIOMM JONSSON

a mass of tetanus

"may lead to impaired judgment and trouble swallowing"

[JUNK] Show her who the REAL man is.

[JUNK] Wish to add more fire into your bedroom life?

[LIKELY JUNK] One big instrument is much better than two
small ones.

[LIKELY JUNK] RedBull fur Ihr bestes Stuck

foiled   back in the high cotton   and she sticks the landing

you are not covered in glory

[JUNK] Only here you can find solution to all your male troubles.

try our delicious _____

[JUNK] Become the best man of her bedroom

soulless, cuckoo, bento   how many ways can I stay
I'm not afraid

Dependence and withdrawal effects (fatigue, loss of appetite, depressed feelings, trouble concentrating)

Some problems can occur while or soon after taking this drug, others come days or weeks afterwards

that's the stuff they've been dying for

[JUNK] Women never leave men who can make them come five times a night. Join this kind of men! You need this thing in your jeans! You ask why? Because this is a little round men's helper that can make woman happy with the fantastic lust and love power that her man suddenly gained. No wonder you need it, price is such low therewith!

I just have four words for you: go away   courting flame

I need a kill switch for   a royal progress

[JUNK] She'll never be disappointed

[LIKELY JUNK] You'll feel yourself with women like Michael Jordan with ball and hoop.

[LIKELY JUNK] Now you don't have to look for women, they will find you themselves.

modesty was never one of your handicaps   mustering an exceptional array

[LIKELY JUNK] Tired of your women leaving your bedroom when you take your pants off?

SANDERS, BLYSOFFE

a kind of mandarin of the third button

use extreme care while doing anything that requires complete
alertness, such as driving a car or operating machinery

we don't have all day   maddening views

you don't know, you don't know anything, and you will never did

[JUNK] You'll call it Peter the Great

I let you win   I let you slip away   on purpose.

[LIKELY JUNK] Women appreciate this quality in men among all
the others.

it's a long war

[JUNK] Boost a growth of your intimate part!

I'm painting abstracts now

[JUNK] She will be the happiest women after sex

what should they know of us   of or of our works

[LIKELY JUNK] A man with a big member has a shining look on
his face

"call your doctor if your throat swells or if you have dry mouth or
constipation"

[JUNK] Get rid of the flatness in your pants just in a few weeks. Your
bed will be attracting women like a magnet

let me make this entirely clear, I won't take yes for an answer

[JUNK] Women will stare at your bulge with their mouth open

revered, tremulous, reticulate, dispassionate blankets, a

Side effects may include

depression

dry mouth

heart attack

high blood pressure

hives

impotence

overstimulation

rapid or pounding heartbeat

seizures

stomach and intestinal disturbances

stroke

weight loss

sudden death

[JUNK] Carry out your main duty as a man—satisfy the women right.

[LIKELY JUNK] 15 ways to make her finish!

~~YCLEPT BEFOULED~~

the ones you were meant toward be with   unseeded
false-echo location

you-just-knew

[JUNK] Some tips to pleasure your lady

OCUSTE FROM

the hail   kicked-off and   I don't even know who you
are anymore

the walking, talking definition of a little goes a long way (

[JUNK] Your manliness has never been bigger.

the holy form factor

Side effects may include

unusual changes in behavior

thoughts of suicide

anxiety

agitation

panic attacks

difficulty sleeping

irritability

hostility

aggressiveness

impulsivity

restlessness

extreme hyperactivity

bruxism (teeth grinding)

a preoccupation with sexual content in some patients, both males and females

deformed so

I just don't think it's right for me   we decided to go in a different direction

[JUNK] You can give your woman more than just medium pleasure.

[JUNK] Make your body real TNT, exploding near girls with passion and desire.

[LIKELY JUNK] 40 Minuten Sex – kein Problem

I feel a feeling coming on

[LIKELY JUNK] Do you feel that you can make lover longer and give much more pleasure to your wife? You certainly can! All you need is a little help to your body. We can give you the solution that helps much better than anything else. Buy it without delay

for our price today is lower than usually.

a lousy machine gun nest

aggression, unpleasant taste, dizziness, disorientation

[JUNK] You will need to buy rubber friends of a bigger size.

the road upon which we ride   I visualize your demise

the inner tension

additional restlessness

the inability to stay still often accompanied by constant pacing
purposeless movements of the feet and legs and marked anxiety

[JUNK] It is always so painful to experience the loss of a girl.

clinically significant weight gain

[JUNK] Girls will call you Largissimo

Unsinging

[JUNK] hoist your lover sexuality with blue pill.

[JUNK] medicinal effect guaranteed. free bonus for every sale

[LIKELY JUNK] If your love warrior is too small, you may lose
this war!

If you are pregnant or plan to become pregnant, inform your doctor
immediately

CRANCH SPELENT

SUBSEQUENT VOTIRS

flu-like symptoms

[JUNK] Get the best shape of your babymaker!

RUCHEM 1957:

[LIKELY JUNK] Avoir energie masculine apparaissent

[JUNK] Vous etes tres chanceux! Nous avons tous a vous seconder a plaisir vos femmes. Notre system adaptable des remises est super—si vous achetez maintenant, vous aurez remises a 15%. Notre livraison est rapide et fiable; il n'y a pas la besoin d'ordonnance

[JUNK] Welcome to the world of big monsters in pants and big possibilities!

[JUNK] Your man's power will return to you like boomerang.

how much less do you need to know?

Suicidal thoughts, or acts

it is the end of days or maybe ofays

[JUNK] Every inch of meat in your pants equals every extra positive feature of your character. Oh wait, who cares about your personality if you have a large device between your legs.

BROOKS FORPHBOR

[JUNK] Strength will fill your Johnson

we always need one neck to choke

[JUNK] Make it reach your knee.

or   a   null   set

mania,

mixed states

rapid cycling and/or psychosis

desperate times call for desperate half-measures

JJIRGEN RECARGHA

"traveler's amnesia"

[LIKELY JUNK] Be a god from her night dreams

ROOF BOOKS

the best in language since 1976

Recent & Selected Titles

• **Flowering Mall** by Brandon Brown. 112 p. $14.95.
• **ONE** by Blake Butler & Vanessa Place.
Assembled by Christopher Higgs. 152 p. $16.95
• **Motes** by Craig Dworkin. 88 p. $14.95
• **Scented Rushes** by Nada Gordon. 104 p. $13.95
• **Accidency** by Joel Kuszai. 120 p. $14.95.
• **Apocalypso** by Evelyn Reilly. 112 p. $14.95
• **Both Poems** by Anne Tardos. 112 p. $14.95
• **Against Professional Secrets** by César Vallejo.
Translated by Joseph Mulligan.
(complete Spanish/English) 104 p. $14.95.
• **Split the Stick: A Minimalist-Divan**
by Mac Wellman. 96 p. $14.95

Roof Books are published by
Segue Foundation
300 Bowery • New York, NY 10012
Visit our website at seguefoundation.com

Roof Books are distributed by
SMALL PRESS DISTRIBUTION
1341 Seventh Street • Berkeley, CA. 94710-1403.
Phone orders: 800-869-7553
spdbooks.org